A Note to Parents and Teachers

Kids can imagine, kids can laugh and kids can learn to read with this exciting new series of first readers. Each book in the Kids Can Read series has been especially written, illustrated and designed for beginning readers. Humorous, easy-to-read stories, appealing characters and engaging illustrations make for books that kids will want to read over and over again.

To make selecting a book easy for kids, parents and teachers, the Kids Can Read series offers three levels based on different reading abilities:

Level 1: Kids Can Start to Read

Short stories, simple sentences, easy vocabulary, lots of repetition and visual clues for kids just beginning to read.

Level 2: Kids Can Read with Help

Longer stories, varied sentences, increased vocabulary, some repetition and visual clues for kids who have some reading skills, but may need a little help.

Level 3: Kids Can Read Alone

Longer, more complex stories and sentences, more challenging vocabulary, language play, minimal repetition and visual clues for kids who are reading by themselves.

With the Kids Can Read series, kids can enter a new and exciting world of reading!

DISCOVER
SPACE

Written by Cynthia Pratt Nicolson
Illustrated by Bill Slavin

Kids Can Press

My thanks go to Dr. Ellis Miner at NASA for generously sharing his expertise on the science of space exploration. Thanks also to staff members at the NASA Jet Proplusion Laboratory and the Johnson Space Center who patiently answered my many questions. — C.P.N.

Kids Can Read ™ Kids Can Read is a trademark of Kids Can Press Ltd.

Kids Can Press acknowledges the financial support of the Government of Ontario, through the Ontario Media Development Corporation's Ontario Book Initiative; the Ontario Arts Council; the Canada Council for the Arts; and the Government of Canada, through the BPIDP, for our publishing activity.

Published in Canada by
Kids Can Press Ltd.
29 Birch Avenue
Toronto, ON M4V 1E2

Published in the U.S. by
Kids Can Press Ltd.
2250 Military Road
Tonawanda, NY 14150

www.kidscanpress.com

Adapted by David MacDonald and Cynthia Pratt Nicolson from the book *Exploring Space*

Edited by Jennifer Stokes
Designed by Sherill Chapman
Educational consultant: Maureen Skinner Weiner, United Synagogue Day School, Willowdale, Ontario

Photo Credits
All photos used courtesy of NASA.

Printed and bound in China

The hardcover edition of this book is smyth sewn casebound.
The paperback edition of this book is limp sewn with a drawn-on cover.

CM 05 0 9 8 7 6 5 4 3 2 1
CM PA 05 0 9 8 7 6 5 4 3 2 1

Library and Archives Canada Cataloguing in Publication

Nicolson, Cynthia Pratt
    Discover space / written by Cynthia Pratt Nicolson ; illustrated by Bill Slavin.

(Kids Can read)
Adaptation of author's Exploring space.
ISBN 1-55337-823-7 (bound).   ISBN 1-55337-824-5 (pbk.)

1. Astronautics — Juvenile literature. 2. Outer space — Exploration — Juvenile literature. I. Slavin, Bill II. Nicolson, Cynthia Pratt. Exploring space. III. Title. IV. Series: Kids Can read (Toronto, Ont.)

TL793.N52 2005   j629.4   C2004-906884-9

Kids Can Press is a **l,◎rus**™ Entertainment company

CONTENTS

LOOKING AT SPACE
FROM EARTH

Space is amazing. It contains more stars than you could count in your whole life.

For hundreds of years, people have looked up at the night sky and wondered, "What's out there in space?"

How did people first learn about space?

Long ago, people watched the sky to see what they could learn about it. They saw the Sun, the Moon and five planets — Mercury, Venus, Mars, Jupiter and Saturn. They also saw many stars.

People noticed that the stars and planets seemed to move slowly. At different times of year, they could be seen in different parts of the sky.

Early people also noticed that the sky changed with the seasons. They could see some stars only in the spring and others only in the fall. In winter, the Sun's path was low in the sky. In summer, it was high overhead. Watching the sky helped people make the first calendars.

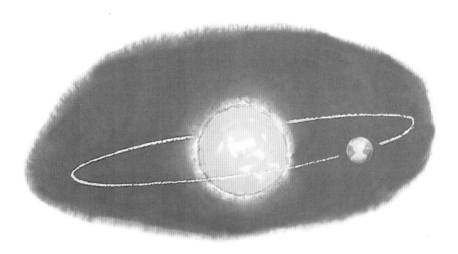

It takes Earth about 365 days to travel around the Sun. That's one year!

Where is space?

Space begins about 120 km (75 mi.) above Earth. If you could drive a car at highway speed straight up into the sky, you would reach space in less than two hours.

Rockets and spaceships travel much faster than cars, so they get to space more quickly.

What is a telescope?

A telescope makes things that are far away look like they are closer. With a telescope, you can see much farther than you can with just your eyes.

About 400 years ago, the scientist Galileo used one of the first telescopes to discover Jupiter's four largest moons.

Long ago, Galileo made discoveries about space using a telescope he made himself.

What did telescopes help us learn about space?

Telescopes helped people discover planets that they couldn't see with just their eyes.

Over time, people learned how to build bigger and better telescopes. Today, scientists use huge telescopes to watch the sky from buildings called observatories.

Today, we have bigger and better telescopes that help us see much farther into space.

OUR SOLAR SYSTEM AND GALAXY

What is the solar system?

The solar system is made up of the Sun and the planets travelling around it. There are nine planets in our solar system. They each travel around the Sun.

Planets circle the Sun in paths called orbits. The arrow is pointing to the planet Earth.

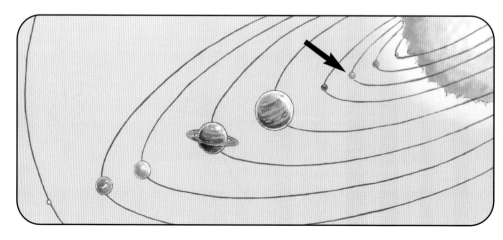

What is a galaxy?

A galaxy is a huge group of stars.
Galaxies are so big, they hold millions
of stars. There are millions of galaxies
in space!

Each spot of light that you see in this photo
is a galaxy far out in space.

Our Sun is part of a galaxy called the Milky Way. There are millions of other stars in the Milky Way.

The Milky Way galaxy is shaped like a pinwheel.

This is a pinwheel shape.

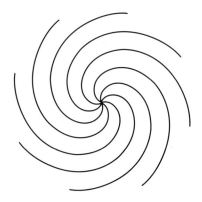

This is a spiral galaxy, much like our own Milky Way galaxy.

ASTRONAUTS IN SPACE

Who was the first person in space?

Yuri Gagarin, from Russia, was the first person to fly into space. His spacecraft blasted off on April 12, 1961. It flew around Earth once before returning home.

This is Yuri Gagarin on the day he flew into space for the first time.

How do astronauts get ready for a space flight?

Astronauts work hard to get ready to fly into space. They exercise every day. They have to learn all about their spacecraft. They also have to learn about what they'll be doing once they get into space.

This astronaut is getting ready for her space flight by trying out her space suit underwater.

What do astronauts wear?

Inside the spacecraft, astronauts wear shirts and pants with many pockets. They wear space suits when they go outside the spacecraft.

On the back of a space suit there is a special machine that lets astronauts fly when they are outside the spacecraft. They can go forward and backward. They can turn around and even flip over!

Space suits protect astronauts from strong sunlight and from bits of dust and rock in space.

What is a space shuttle?

A space shuttle is a special kind of spacecraft. It looks like an airplane with rockets attached. These rockets help the space shuttle fly from Earth into space.

Most spacecraft can be used for only one flight. A space shuttle can be used for many flights.

Two rockets give the space shuttle *Discovery* enough power to fly into space.

What is a space station?

A space station is a place where astronauts can live and work in space. The first space station was called *Mir*. It was sent into space from Russia in 1971.

The International Space Station is being built slowly over time. The first part of it was built on Earth, and then it was sent into space. Astronauts work on building other parts of the space station while it is in space.

This is the International Space Station. The large black rectangles collect energy from the Sun to give power to the equipment on the space station.

What is it like to live on a space station?

Sleeping: There isn't enough room for beds in a space station. The astronauts sleep in sleeping bags that they need to put away every morning.

Eating: Most of the food is frozen or dried so it won't spoil. For drinks, astronauts add water to a powder mix.

Keeping clean: There is no bathtub in a space station. Astronauts use a wet sponge to keep their bodies clean.

Two astronauts share a meal on the International Space Station.

EXPLORING THE MOON

The race to the Moon

Scientists in the United States of America and in Russia were once in a race to see which country would be the first to land astronauts on the Moon.

This is the Moon, as seen from space.

Who was the first person on the Moon?

The United States won the race to land astronauts on the moon.

On July 20, 1969, Neil Armstrong became the first person to walk on the Moon. Astronaut Buzz Aldrin was with him. People on Earth watched on TV as Neil Armstrong took his first footstep onto the Moon.

Neil Armstrong took this photo of Buzz Aldrin and their landing craft on the Moon.

What did the first astronauts on the Moon do?

The astronauts collected Moon rocks and Moon dust for scientists to study. They also put up the flag of the United States.

Later trips to the Moon

Astronauts from the United States went to the Moon five more times after the first astronauts landed there.

In later trips to the Moon, astronauts used a "Moon buggy" to drive around on the surface of the Moon.

The "Moon buggy" let astronauts travel around and explore the Moon.

EXPLORING OTHER PLANETS IN OUR SOLAR SYSTEM

What is a space probe?

A space probe is a spacecraft that doesn't carry any astronauts. It can stay in space much longer than a spacecraft with humans on board.

Space probes help us learn about places that are too far away for astronauts to explore.

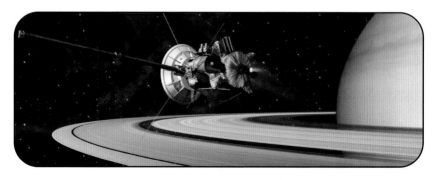

This is an artist's picture of the Cassini space probe travelling around Saturn.

How do space probes work?

A space probe is a kind of robot. Scientists on Earth control the space probe by sending signals to tell it what to do.

What do space probes do?

Different space probes are made to do different things. Most space probes take pictures and send them back to Earth. Some probes land on a planet and collect soil and rocks for scientists to study. Space probes help us learn many things about other planets.

This photo of Jupiter was taken by the Cassini space probe.

Journey to Mars

Astronauts have never landed on Mars. But space probes have helped us to learn more about this planet.

First, scientists sent space probes to fly by Mars and take pictures of it. After that, space probes were sent to circle around Mars. These probes took pictures of many different parts of the planet.

In 1976, the *Viking 1* space probe became the first to land on Mars.

The soil on Mars is reddish brown. That's why Mars is sometimes called "the red planet."

Robot rovers on Mars

The first space probes to land on Mars couldn't move from where they landed. Scientists later invented robots called "rovers" that can travel around on Mars. These rovers are controlled by computers and by signals that scientists send from Earth. The rovers can even do experiments with the rocks and soil on Mars!

This is an artist's picture of the Mars Exploration Rover on the surface of Mars.

What have we learned from space probes?

Over 40 space probes have explored the planets in our solar system. Here are some of the amazing things that scientists have learned from space probes:

The planet Saturn has large rings around it. Photos from space probes showed that these big rings are made of many smaller rings.

Space probes have shown us that the planet Jupiter is surrounded by fast-moving clouds.

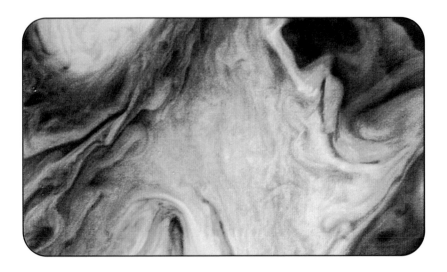

This picture from a space probe showed scientists what the land on Venus looks like.

EXPLORING OUTSIDE OUR SOLAR SYSTEM

The Hubble Space Telescope

In 1990, scientists sent the Hubble Space Telescope into space. This telescope is able to see things that we can't see from telescopes on Earth. The Hubble Space Telescope lets scientists see more clearly into outer space.

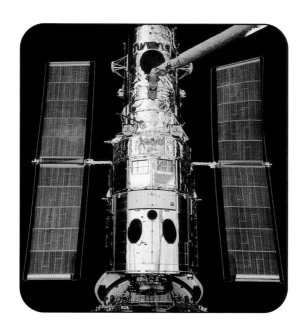

This is the Hubble Space Telescope.

Fixing the Hubble Space Telescope

The Hubble Space Telescope started sending photos back to earth. But the photos were fuzzy! Scientists learned that there was a problem with the telescope. In 1993, astronauts went into space to fix it.

Astronauts work to fix the Hubble Space Telescope.

The two photos below show the same galaxy. The Hubble Space Telescope took both photos.

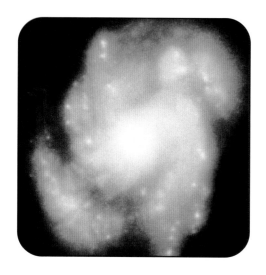

This fuzzy photo was taken when the Hubble Space Telescope was first sent into space.

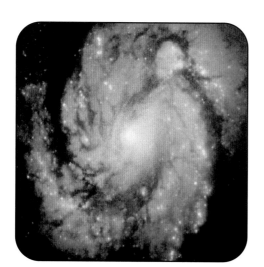

This clear photo was taken after the Hubble Space Telescope was fixed.

EXPLORING SPACE IN THE FUTURE

Will people ever live in space?

Astronauts have lived on space stations for months at a time. Sometime in the future, we may build places where people could live on the Moon or on Mars.

Will people ever travel to the stars?

The closest star to our solar system is very, very far away. It is so far away that none of our spacecraft could travel to it.

Maybe one day we'll build a spacecraft that can travel to other parts of our galaxy. For now, scientists can only dream about a trip to the stars.

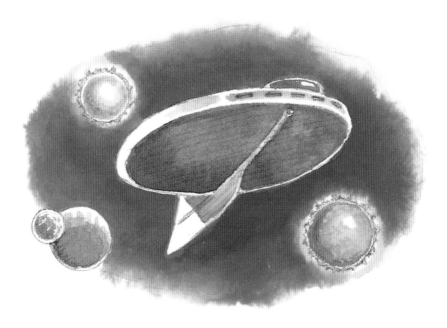